$12.95

Ancient Ships on American Shores

Written and Illustrated by

Michael Custode

Researched and Co-written by

Patricia Presti

Three Trees Press

Discovery Series

Introduction

> "Surely there cannot now be any question ... there were visitors to the New World from the Old in historic or even prehistoric time before 1492."
>
> *Society for American Archeology, May 1968**

Asia

Chinese

Who discovered America first?

Many people still believe that Christopher Columbus was the first Old World explorer to set foot in the New World when he landed on one of the Bahama Islands in 1492. Although Columbus helped to open up these vast "new" lands to Europeans (for which he will always have a place in the history books), he did not discover America — he *rediscovered* it. Many groups of people travelled to the Americas hundreds and perhaps even thousands of years before Columbus.

People have lived in the Americas for at least 20,000 to 30,000 years. Some paleontologists (people who study prehistoric life) claim to have proof of human presence in America as far back as 250,000 years ago. They believe that these people came to North America via the Bering Strait, between Alaska and the present-day U.S.S.R. However, these people may have arrived in ships. After all, the ships of the Phoenicians, built 3,000 years before Columbus's day, were larger than his and better adapted to cross the sea!

Early explorers visited the New World at various times. Some of them returned to their native lands with stories of a mysterious land beyond the vast ocean. But others made their homes in the new land. Their influences can be traced in the Indian cultures of North and South America.

Legends from both the Old and New Worlds suggest that early sailors landed on American shores 5,000 years ago, rather than 500 years ago. These voyages originated in Asia, Africa, and Europe. Sailors from China and Japan, from the Mali Empire in Africa,

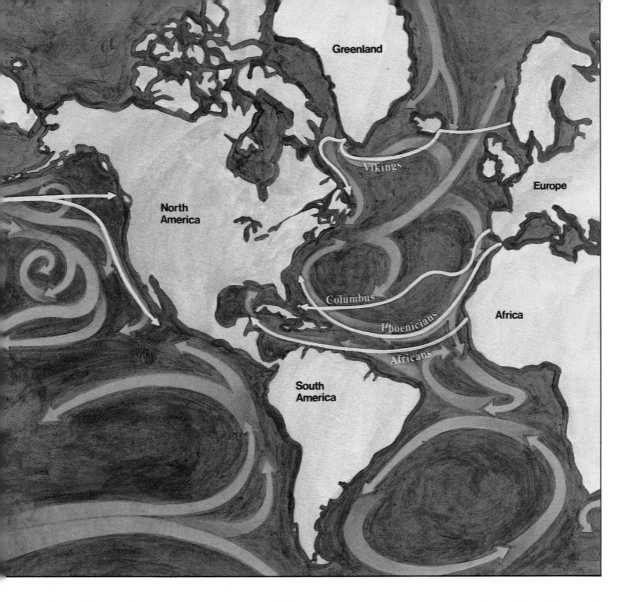

from the Mediterranean countries of Phoenicia, Libya, and Iberia (Spain), and even Vikings and Celts all landed on American shores before 1492.

Much of the information in this book is still being disputed by scientists. However, we believe that the groups of people mentioned on the following pages actually reached American shores. You are invited to make up

your own mind, perhaps by reading some of the books and articles listed at the end of this book.

The map shows the routes by which these early explorers might have reached the New World. In the following pages, we will examine these ancient travellers in more detail.

*As quoted by Ivan van Sertima in *They Came Before Columbus* (New York: Random House, 1976).

Merchants of the Mediterranean

The ancient Phoenicians, a merchant, sea-going people, came from the area we now know as Lebanon. They may have sailed to America around 1000 B.C. At that time the Phoenicians were great traders. They traded goods such as the purple dye of the Canary Islands, British tin, African gold, and probably American copper. Their "tubby" merchant ships were suited to trans-Atlantic travel; they relied on wind rather than oars for power. They also carried small crews and had more storage space for provisions than the sleek Phoenician warships did.

By 900 B.C., the Phoenicians ruled a string of colonies along the shores of the Mediterranean, from Malta and North Africa to the Iberian peninsula. These oceangoing mariners had learned through experience that, after leaving Gibraltar, it was best to sail in westerly arcs to their destination rather than follow the shoreline. It is possible that sailing in wider and wider arcs eventually brought them to America.

Evidence for the Phoenician presence in America exists in both literature and archaeology. The earliest historical reference to the lands west of the Strait of Gibraltar comes from the Greek historian Herodotus in 5 B.C. He wrote about the trading methods used for customers who did not speak the same language as the Phoenicians.

Four hundred stone slabs were recently found in Pennsylvania. Each of these slabs was etched with Punic writing, the writing of the Phoenicians. Some archaeologists believe that Phoenician traders may have arrived in North America, settled there, and eventually intermarried with the Wabanaki Indians of New England. There is also archaeological evidence, based on tools unearthed in Michigan and along the Mississippi, that Phoenicians and other Mediterranean people mined copper in those areas.

Another group that might have travelled to America at this time was the Iberians, who were Basques and Celts. They came from the area we now know as Spain. The first accidental trans-Atlantic drifting of the Iberians may have been as early as 3400 B.C., and the first Celtiberian cultures are believed to have reached North America between 800 and 100 B.C.

Libyans and Egyptians also may have visited America at this time. The similarity between Egyptian hieroglyphics and the writing of the Micmac Indians makes this seem possible. Another interesting fact is the recent discovery of potatoes in an ancient Egyptian tomb. Since potatoes were not known in the Old World before the 16th century, the ancient Egyptians may have imported them from America.

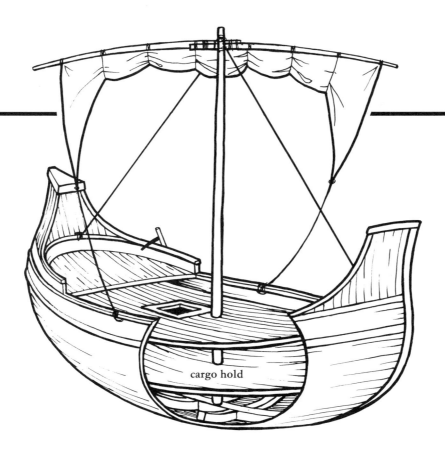

cargo hold

MEDITERRANEAN SHIPS

Few details are known about ancient Mediterranean ships. Since so much trading was done by travel at sea, these vessels must have been both rugged and seaworthy. The largest merchant ships probably were about 60 metres (200 feet) long and able to carry several hundred tonnes of cargo. They were not very graceful; these round, wide ships probably were guided by a crude rudder. Merchant ships generally relied on wind and sail to travel. Since rowing sometimes was necessary, most ships were built to accommodate oarsmen.

OVERLEAF ILLUSTRATION

The following illustration shows Mediterranean merchant vessels docked on the shores of an inland American river. As crews unload the ships, one of the merchants trades with a group of North American Indians. In the background is the entrance to a copper mine.

The Chinese

Chinese and American Indian legends, and artifacts found near the West Coast of North America, give some evidence that the ancient Chinese sailed ships called junks, or just simple bamboo rafts, across the Pacific Ocean.

The West Coast Indians have a story about the "Eaters of Maggots." This legend dates from before the arrival of the first Europeans to the West Coast, under Captain James Cook, in 1778. To a people who had never seen anyone eat rice before, this name for the Chinese makes sense. These same West Coast Indians were unique in their clothes, which suggested Asian influence. They also wore a woven hat instead of the usual headdress. Remarkably, the hat is very similar to those worn by Chinese sailors until the 1800s.

According to one Chinese legend, a Buddhist priest named Hwui Shan and four other monks left that country in A.D. 458 on a journey eastward. They eventually landed at a place they called "Fu-Sang," about 20,000 li (11,500 kilometres or 7,000 miles) east of China. Fu-Sang, probably the region around present-day Southern California and Mexico, was described by Hwui Shan as a country where a "peaceful people" lived. These people knew of gold and silver but did not value them highly, and they were not familiar with iron at all.

Living in simple wooden dwellings, the natives used the "fu-sang" tree to make food, clothing, and paper. This tree might be the aloe plant. According to Hwui Shan, the natives filled ditches with "water-silver." We know that the West Coast Indians filled pits with *eulachon*, a silver-coloured fish. In short, Hwui Shan seems to have given a very detailed report on the habits and people of America in the 5th century.

Chinese literature also confirms the possibility of early trans-Pacific travel to America. The oldest Chinese manuscript, the *Shan Hai King* (*Classic of Mountain and Seas*), dates from about 2250 B.C. The last book of the four-volume series, *The Classic of the Eastern Mountains*, gives a detailed survey of North America from Manitoba to Mexico, including an accurate description of the Grand Canyon!

Scuba divers in California have discovered large boulders, weighing from 70 to 320 kilograms (150 to 700 pounds) each, off the Palos Verdes peninsula in Los Angeles. These rocks may be ancient anchors used by the Chinese. The possibility of East Asians visiting American shores in ancient times has increased with the unearthing of ancient Japanese artifacts and pottery in Mexico, Ecuador, and British Columbia in the past century.

From time to time, abandoned or runaway junks have been found on the West Coast, driven there by the strong pull of the Japanese Current. The current, originating off the coast of Japan and flowing across the North Pacific Ocean, could easily have brought ships and explorers to American

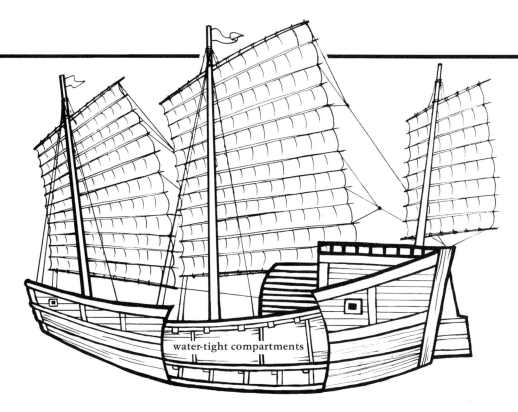

water-tight compartments

shores in ancient times. The North Equatorial Current, which flows from North America to Asia, may have brought them home again.

CHINESE SHIPS

The Chinese junk has changed little over thousands of years. Although it is a clumsy-looking ship, the junk has one of the best seafaring safety records. The ancient Chinese devised many important naval improvements. Their junks used a stern rudder, while in Europe sailors still used an oar for steering their ships. Junks also had watertight compartments for cargo and living quarters. For navigating, the Chinese used an early form of compass.

OVERLEAF ILLUSTRATION

The following illustration shows a Chinese junk approaching the shore of British Columbia in A.D. 500. Hwui Shan, thought to be the first person to land on the West Coast from China, commented that "the residence of the kings is adorned ... with many beautiful objects about the dwellings." The villages described by Hwui Shan are much like those found on the West Coast at that time.

The Vikings

During the Viking era (A.D. 800 to 1100), Norwegian Vikings set out to conquer many lands. They travelled vast distances, from Scotland to the Mediterranean Sea, and eventually to North America.

The Viking discovery of North America was a result of a series of westward journeys. The Vikings first discovered Iceland in the middle of the 9th century. The great Viking explorer Eirik the Red settled in Iceland but was later banished as an outlaw. In A.D. 982, Eirik sailed to Greenland, which had been sighted some years before. Later he brought settlers to Greenland. By the 13th century, 4,000 Nordic people lived in Greenland. Since less than 500 kilometres (300 miles) separates the shores of Greenland and North America, it is not surprising that the Vikings eventually reached North America.

Two Viking sagas, *The Greenlanders' Saga* and *Eirik the Red's Saga*, describe voyages to North America.

In A.D. 986, Bjarni Herjolfssen sailed from Iceland to Greenland. Lost in bad weather, Bjarni sighted the shores of America before reaching Greenland. Later, the son of Eirik the Red, Leif Eiriksson, left Greenland with 35 others and sailed in search of the land that Bjarni had seen. Leif came to a place he called "Helluland" (Baffin Island); he then travelled south to "Markland" (Labrador). From there he sailed further south, finally discovering "Vinland," which is probably Newfoundland. The Vikings spent a year there, before returning to Greenland.

Leif Eiriksson's expedition was followed by three more. All of them stayed in the shelters that Leif's men had built. They both traded and fought with the natives. During one of the battles, the Vikings sighted a unique creature among the attacking natives, which they called a "uniped." Curiously enough, ancient Irish legends mention "unipeds" as being among the original inhabitants of Ireland.

Near the small fishing village of L'Anse aux Meadows, a Viking settlement has been excavated. It dates from around A.D. 1000, which is about the same time that Leif Eiriksson would have discovered Vinland. It consists of eight or nine structures, including a blacksmith's forge, a kiln, two outdoor cooking pits, and four or five boatsheds. These may not have been built by Leif Eiriksson and his crew, but they are the most positive evidence that Vikings settled in North America before Columbus's time.

The site at L'Anse aux Meadows is sponsored by UNESCO as a part of the cultural heritage of mankind, as important as the Egyptian pyramids in its significance.

VIKING SHIPS

The Vikings were skilled shipbuilders and navigators. It is easy to recognize their slender, graceful ships. There were several types of these wooden vessels, including warships, merchant ships, and fishing boats. They usually had one square sail. They also had oarports so that the crew could row when the wind died down. Steering was provided by a side rudder.

The warship, or longship as it is often called, was a long, narrow vessel built for speed. The prow was usually decorated with a carved animal head. One of the largest Viking warships found was 28 metres (92 feet) long and 4.5 metres (15 feet) wide. It could carry between fifty and sixty men.

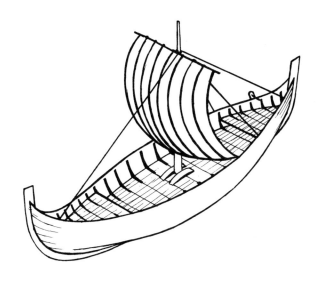

The merchant ship was built to carry cargo and, although it was not as fast as a warship, it was very efficient. It was deeper and wider than the warship and had an open hold for cargo, which often included farm animals.

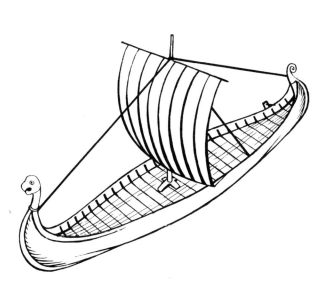

OVERLEAF ILLUSTRATION

The following illustration shows how the Viking settlement at L'Anse aux Meadows may have looked. The settlers have brought livestock, supplies, and tools to their new home. In the background are several buildings with earth walls and thatched or wooden roofs. Beside them are several boatsheds.

Black Africans

Some ancient sculpted stone heads were found in Mexico in 1862. These heads date from as early as 800 to 700 B.C. They were especially common among the Olmec tribe of Central America, who lived in the jungle along the Gulf Coast. At La Venta, Mexico, the religious centre of the Olmec tribe, there are four huge African heads up to 3 metres (9 feet) tall and weighing 40 tonnes each. Seven other stone heads have been found near La Venta.

In 1975, scholars from the Smithsonian Institution unearthed two African male skeletons in the Virgin Islands; the soil in which the skeletons were discovered was dated to A.D. 1250. Many clay, stone, and gold portraits of Africans, dating from 700 B.C. onward, have been found in Central America. The Negroid features of these sculptures are unmistakable.

The court tradition of the Mali Kingdom, on the central-west coast of Africa, and documents in Cairo tell of two Atlantic trips decreed by the great African king Abubakari II. In 1310, the king ordered 200 masterboats and 200 supply boats to set out for the "great sea of darkness." Their mission was to determine whether the ocean was the end of the world or if there were new lands to conquer. Abubakari himself set sail on the Atlantic in the next year. Neither of these two fleets returned. However, many of the African-related artifacts found in Mexico date from the time of these African voyages.

The currents of the Atlantic Ocean move with great power and swiftness from Africa to America. They could easily carry an African ship across the Atlantic. One branch of the North Equatorial Current could have taken a ship from the North African or West African coast right into the Gulf of Mexico.

Only a few years after Columbus sailed to the New World, Africans were discovered in the Americas. Fray Gregoria Garcia, a Dominican priest, found Africans living in Colombia. The explorer Balboa found Africans as Indian prisoners near the Isthmus of Darien in Central America. These two areas are terminal points for the trans-Atlantic currents that could easily have brought Africans to the Americas.

Olmec Negroid stone head

Later, large boats were made of planks that were held together by rope (palm fibre) instead of nails. These could be rowed or equipped with a sail.

OVERLEAF ILLUSTRATION

The following illustration shows Abubakari's fleet, as it might have looked, approaching the coast of Central America. The boats are like those found on the East Coast of Africa, where Asian seafarers settled. Eventually they migrated to the Central West Coast; their descendants might have helped to build Abubakari's fleets.

AFRICAN SHIPS

It is difficult to say what type of ship the Africans might have used to make a journey to the New World. The earliest boat was a dugout canoe. It was simply a hollowed-out log, and its size was limited by the size of the log. But dugouts were often extended by attaching planks to the log. Carrying cargo became much easier, and square sails provided the power.

Christopher Columbus

In the 15th century, Europe was looking for a new route to the East Indies. The Europeans had received spices, perfumes, and rich fabrics from the Indies, but the Turks had closed off the Meditteranean trade routes to the East. Some people believed a new route was to the south, around the tip of Africa. Others thought it was to the west, across the Atlantic Ocean. The merchant-seamen of medieval Europe did not realize that a whole continent lay across the Atlantic, and that a direct passage to the Orient was impossible.

Christopher Columbus became one of the many explorers who were sure that a western route led to the Orient. It is possible that Columbus had heard rumours from Africa or from Arabs or Turks of a land in that direction. The "Piri Re'is" maps, found recently in a depository and which predate Columbus's voyage, show the coastlines of the Americas and other parts of the world, including Antarctica. Some people speculate that Columbus himself used such a map, or a fragment of one, as a guide for his voyage, quite unaware of what it actually portrayed.

In 1484, Columbus was granted an audience with King John II of Portugal. Columbus tried to convince the king that the best route to the Orient was to the west. The king and his experts thought Columbus was boastful and untrustworthy. Since they believed that the quickest route was south, around Africa, they refused to support Columbus's proposed trip.

Finally, in 1486, Columbus convinced Queen Isabella of Spain that he could cross the Atlantic to reach the Orient. He asked for three ships and supplies to reach his goal. After long talks, his request was granted.

On August 3, 1492, Columbus sailed west, ignoring the experts who thought he would never reach his goal. Naturally, he didn't reach the Orient. On October 12, he reached the Bahamas, thinking he had reached the East Indies. He had "discovered" America, but didn't realize it. Columbus made three more trips to America, but he still insisted he had discovered the Orient. He thought Cuba was Japan, and later he decided it was part of China. He visited the islands of the West Indies, Venezuela, and Central America, but apparently never understood that he had encountered a completely independent continent.

Columbus demonstrated the existence of sea routes between Europe and America; but the explorers who came after him were the ones who eventually proved to Europe that the Americas were, indeed, "new" continents.

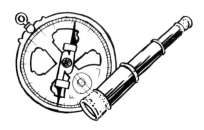

CHRISTOPER COLUMBUS'S SHIPS

During the 100 years before Columbus's voyages, Europeans had been studying shipping and navigating to improve their knowledge. This interest was especially concentrated in the western seafaring countries such as Portugal and Spain. The knowledge they gained greatly improved European ships.

In the 15th century, with a great search on for new trade routes, a small wooden merchant ship called a caravel was developed. Caravels were wooden merchants ships about 18 to 21 metres (60 to 70 feet) long, with a capacity of about 70 tonnes. Columbus made his famous trip in three caravels: the *Nina*, the *Pinta*, and the *Santa Maria*. Columbus's flagship, the *Santa Maria*, was a slightly larger caravel, about 29 metres long and 8 metres wide (95 feet by 26 feet). These ships usually had living quarters above deck and cargo holds below. The sails were not easy to handle; they required a large crew to handle them.

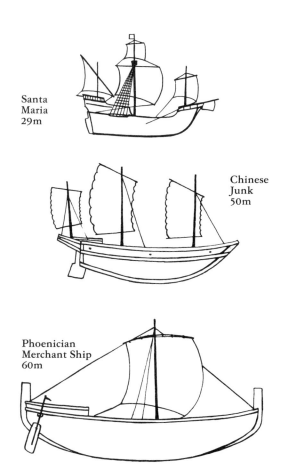

Santa
Maria
29m

Chinese
Junk
50m

Phoenician
Merchant Ship
60m

OVERLEAF ILLUSTRATION

The following illustration shows Columbus setting foot in the New World at the Bahamas. The land seemed to be deserted at first; the natives were hidden in the bushes. Curious about newcomers, they eventually came out to greet Columbus and his crew. In the background the three ships, the Pinta, *the* Santa Maria, *and the* Nina, *are moored in the bay.*

Suggested Reading

Ashe, Geoffrey *et al. The Quest for America.* New York: Praeger Publishers, 1971.

Bass, George F. (ed.). *A History of Sea-faring.* New York: Walker & Co., 1972.

Boyle, Robert W. "Cartier was Likely a Latecomer." *Canadian Geographic*, Oct./Nov. 1984, vol. 104, no. 5.

Bradley, Michael. *Black Discovery of America.* Toronto: Personal Library, 1981.

Caley, Peter. "Canada's Chinese Columbus." *The Beaver*, Spring 1983.

Donovan, Frank A. *The Vikings.* New York: Harper & Row, 1964.

Fell, Barry. *America B.C.* New York: Simon and Schuster, 1976.

Fell, Barry. *Bronze Age America.* Toronto: Little, Brown & Co., 1982.

Gordon, Cyrus H. *Before Columbus.* New York: Crown Publishers, 1971.

Grant, Neil. *The Discoverers.* New York: Arco Publishing, 1979.

Gwynne, Peter. "Who Discovered America Second?" *World Book Encyclopedia Year Book.* Chicago: Field Enterprises Educational Corp., 1977.

Hapgood, Charles H. *Maps of the Ancient Sea Kings.* New York: E.P. Dutton, 1979.

Hitchings, Francis. *The World Atlas of Mysteries.* London: Pan Books, 1981.

Holard, Hjalmar R. *Explorations in America Before Columbus.* New York: Twayne Publishers, 1959.

Johnstone, Paul. *The Sea-craft of Pre-history.* Cambridge, Mass.: Harvard University Press, 1980.

Kemp, Peter (ed.). *Encyclopedia of Ships and Sea-faring.* New York: Crown Publishers, 1980.

Klint-Jensen, Ole, and Svenolov Ehren. *The World of the Vikings.* New York: Robert B. Luce Inc., 1980.

Landstrom, Bjorn. *Bold Voyages and Great Explorers.* New York: Doubleday & Co., 1964.

Leitch, Michael. *The Romance of Sail.* London: Hamlyn Publishing, 1975.

Lillard, Charles. "Ocean Bridge, Ocean Barrier." *Horizon Canada*, Oct. 1984, vol. 1, no. 10.

Maclellan, David. "Who Discovered America First?" *Canadian Geographic*, June/July 1984, vol. 104, no. 3.

McGhee, Robert. "Early Arrivals." *Canadian Heritage Magazine*, May 1981.

Oleson, Tryggvi. *Early Voyages and Northern Approaches.* Toronto: McClelland and Stewart, 1963.

Pohl, Frederick J. *Viking Explorers.* New York: Thomas T. Crowell Co., 1966.

Trento, Salvatore Michael. *The Search for Lost America.* Toronto: Penguin Books, 1978.

Tunis, Edwin. *Oars, Sails and Steam.* New York: World Publishing Co., 1952.

van Sertima, Ivan. *They Came Before Columbus.* New York: Random House, 1976.

Vernon, John. *The First Explorers.* London: B.T. Batsford Ltd., 1978.

"Who Were the First Canadians?" *Canadian Heritage Magazine*, May 1981.

Canadian Cataloguing in Publication Data

Custode, Michael.
    Ancient ships on American shores
    (Discovery series)

ISBN 0-88823-113-X (bound). - ISBN 0-88823-115-6 (pbk.)

1. Ships - History - Juvenile literature.
2. America - Discovery and exploration
    - Juvenile literature.   I. Title.
    II. Series: Discovery series (Toronto, Ont.)

VM150.C87 1986   j387.2'09   C86-093659-7

ISBN 0-88823-115-6 pb
ISBN 0-88823-113-X hc

© 1986 Three Trees Press Inc.
Text and illustrations by Michael Custode
All rights reserved
Published by Three Trees Press
2 Silver Avenue, 2nd Floor
Toronto, Ontario M6R 3A2

Printed and bound in Canada

Published with the assistance of the
Canada Council and the Ontario Arts Council